On a Scotch Bard

An Illustrated Life of
Robert Burns

Keith Mitchell

Published by Neil Wilson Publishing Ltd
309 The Pentagon Centre
36 Washington Street
GLASGOW G3 8AZ
Tel: 041—221—1117
Fax: 041—221—5363

A catalogue record for this book is available from The British Library
ISBN 1-897784-22-8

Typeset in Bookman and Linoscript by
Face to Face Design Services, Glasgow

Printed in Musselburgh by Scotprint Ltd

On a Scotch Bard

An Illustrated Life of
Robert Burns

Keith Mitchell

Neil Wilson Publishing, Glasgow

There was a lad was born in Kyle,
But whatna day o' whatna style
I doubt it's hardly worth the while
To be sae nice wi' Robin.

There was a Lad, 1785.

William Burncs, a gardener from Kincardineshire, took his wife, Agnes Brown from Maybole in Ayrshire to the cottage he had built in 1757, and there Scotland's national poet, Robert Burns was born on 25 January 1759. A few days after his birth, the wind damaged the house, and Agnes and her baby son went to stay with a neighbour until the

damage was repaired. Burns wrote of it years later.

Our monarch's hindmost year but ane
Was five-and-twenty days begun;
'Twas then a blast o' Janwar win'
Blew hansel in on Robin.

There was a Lad, 1785.

The young Burns learnt something of the Scots folk tradition at his mother's knee, as she sang while going about the dairy. In common with many of her class, Agnes although barely able to read and unable to write, was a great preserver of the oral tradi-

Agnes Burnes 1723~1820

tion; indeed, one of her favourite airs must have made a deep impression on young Robert —

Kissin' is the key o' love
An' clappin' is the lock,
An' makin Q's the best thing
That e'er a young thing got.

Little did she know that eventually her son would rescue Scots folk-music from the bawdy depths to which it had sunk.

A frequent visitor to Alloway was Betty Davidson, a relative who helped Agnes around the farm, and Burns was to recall of her that she had "...the largest collection in the county of tales and songs concerning devils, ghosts, fairies, brownies, witches, warlocks, spunkies, kelpies, elf-candles, deil-lights, wraiths, apparitions, cantraips, giants, inchanted towers, dragons and other trumpery." She was also "...remarkable for her ignorance, credulity and superstition... This cultivated the latent seeds of Poesy."

7

Little is known of the poet's early life, although it is reasonable to suppose he and his brothers and sisters would have played on the banks of the River Doon and around the fields and market garden at Alloway.

Three other children were born at the clay biggin, Gilbert (1760), Agnes (1762) and Annabella (1764). These would be followed by William (1767), John (1769) and Isabella (1771).

Although Robert's father had a liberal outlook, he was indoctrinating his eldest son in strict Calvinist orthodoxy, in keeping with the mood of the times. Burns describes himself at this time — "I was a good deal noted for a retentive memory, a stubborn, sturdy something in my disposition, and an enthusiastic idiot-piety, because I was then but a child."

By Acts of Parliament of 1633 and 1634,

8

every parish in Scotland was to provide public schools. In practice, however, the requirement was rarely met and education was in the hands of the parents. So when the teacher, Mr. Campbell, left Alloway school, William Burnes interviewed John Murdoch, an 18 year old teacher, and a bargain was struck. Murdoch later recalled of his pupils, Robert and his younger brother Gilbert — "They both made a rapid progress in reading, and a tolerable progress in writing. ... Robert

Ye banks and braes o' bonie Doon,
How can ye bloom sae fresh and fair?
How can ye chant, ye little birds,
And I sae weary fu' o' care!
Ye Banks and Braes, 1791

Auld Brig o' Doon

and Gilbert were ... at the upper end of the class, even when ranged with boys by far their seniors. I attempted to teach them a little church-music. Here they were left behind by all the rest of the school. Robert's countenance was generally grave, and expressive of a serious, contemplative and thoughtful mind."

The literature Robert came across at school show the origins of his later difficulties in shifting between Scots vernacular and the high flown Augustan style, from Milton, Dryden etc. Two books in particular caught young Robert's imagination, *The History of Sir William Wallace* and *The Life of Hannibal*, the former pouring "a Scottish prejudice into my veins which will boil along there till the flood-gates of life shut in eternal rest."

My father was a Farmer upon the Carrick border O,

And carefully he bred me in decency and order O;

He bade me act a manly part, though I had ne' er a farthing O,

For without an honest manly heart, no man was worth regarding O.

My Father was a Farmer, 1782.

Whitsun 1766 saw the Burnes family move to the 70 acre farm at Mount Oliphant, two miles from Alloway. The boys continued their education at Alloway until the early part of 1768, when the needs of the farm required their full attention. The farm proved to be a millstone around the collective family neck, Gilbert described it as, "...almost the very poorest soil I know of in a state of cultivation". Robert remembered it as "The cheerless gloom of a hermit with the unceasing

Mount Oliphant

11

moil of a galley slave...", for with his father being able to hire no farm servants, Robert became his chief labourer.

No help, nor hope, nor view had I, nor person to befriend me O;
So I must toil, and sweat and moil, and labour to sustain me O;
To plough and sow, to reap and mow, my father bred me early O;
For one, he said, to labour bred, was a match for fortune fairly O.
My Father was a Farmer, 1782.

In between bouts of hard work and meagre diet, Robert managed to fit in some further stabs at education spending some time improving his handwriting in the summer of 1772 at Dalrymple, and learning English grammar and a little French with Murdoch at Ayr, in 1773.

Equally important is the first recorded poem penned by Burns, inspired by a girl, Helen Blair, who worked beside the 15-year-old Robert, gathering the harvest. He described her as "...a bonie, sweet, sonsie lass" and confessed that his heart "beat such a furious ratann when I looked and fingered over her hand, to pick out the nettle-stings and thistles".

Burns, on enquiring about an air which Nelly sang, discovered that its author was a small country laird's son, and Robert saw no reason why "...I might not rhyme as well as he, for excepting smearing sheep and casting peats, his father living in the moors, he had no more Scholarcraft than I had."

She dresses aye sae clean and neat,
Both decent and genteel;
And then there's something in her gait,
Gars onie dress look weel.

O, Once I lov'd a bonie lass, 1773.

The problems surrounding the farm were by now coming to a head. The ground was still unyielding and there was only William and his two sons to work them. Provost Fergusson, from whom the farm was rented, had died and his estate

was in the hands of a factor. "My indignation yet boils", wrote Burns "at the recol-
lection of the scoundrel tyrant's insolent,
threatening epistles, which used to set us
all in tears". In *The Twa Dogs*, written in
1786, Burns sets Luath, his own collie,
and Caesar, a rich man's dog, in conver-
sation on the different lifestyles of poor
and wealthy, recalling the factor —

Poor tenant bodies, scant o' cash,

How they maun thole a factor's smash;

He'll stamp an threaten, curse an swear,

He'll apprehend them, poind their gear.

The Twa Dogs, 1786

Amid this, Robert was sent to Kirko-
swald to learn "mensuration, surveying
and dialling" at Hugh Rodger's school. A
girl by the name of Peggy Thomson who
lived next to the school, "overset my Trig-
onometry, and set me off in a Tangent
from the sphere of my studies". His stay
there gave him a chance to observe mankind, where he saw "scenes of swaggering
riot" among the smugglers and sailors.

This brought his schooling days to a close and in 1777, with Robert now 18 and finally rid of Mount Oliphant, they moved to Lochlea, or Lochlie, as it was then spelled, near Tarbolton. When the family actually moved into Lochlea, they found that, once again, it was a bad bargain. It was not even sealed in writing from their new landlord, David McLure Inevitably, for the first four years it was all hard toil for William and his sons but Robert recorded that "For four years we lived comfortably here", so it must have been worthwhile.

At Lochlea, Robert's first real difference with his father occurred — "...to give my manners a brush, I went to a country dancing school. My father had an unaccountable antipathy

Lochlea

15

against these meetings; and my going was, what to this hour I repent, in absolute defiance of his commands". Burns also felt that from then on his father, "took a kind of dislike to me". By now 20 and having spent his teenage years working himself to the bone, living off an insufficient diet which led eventually to his early death, Robert must have felt entitled to some of the social recreation which the nearby town of Tarbolton could offer. Burns increased the scope of his reading, including a *Collection of English Songs*, also works of Pope, Sterne, Henry Mackenzie and the bogus Ossian epics. Perhaps even more importantly, he read poems by his fellow Scot Robert Fergusson, who died in an asylum after a fall involving head injuries. Like Burns, he wrote in the vernacular and Robert based his *Cotter's Saturday Night* on Fergusson's *Farmers Ingle*; *Holy Fair* on *Leith Races* and *The Twa Dogs* on *Mutual Complaint of Plainstanes and Causey.*

In 1787, Burns erected a tombstone over Fergusson's grave, part of which read —

This humble tribute with a tear he gives,
A brother Bard, who no more can bestow:
But dear to fame thy Song immortal lives,
A nobler monument than Art can show.

It was during the time at Lochlea that Burns' poetry became more and more influenced by the Scots tongue through Fergusson, Allan Ramsay (author of *The Gentle Shepherd*) among others and in a style which was becoming much admired by some of Scotland's more genteel society, especially ladies of aristocratic families. Robert was by now making new friends in and around Tarbolton, such as David Sillar from Spittleside,

Robert Fergusson

1750 -1774

17

Haud to the Muse, my dainty Davie:
The warl' may play you mony a shavie;
But for the muse, she'll never leave ye,
Tho e'er sae puir,
Na, even tho limpin wi the spavie
Frae door to door.

Second Epistle to Davie, 1785

John Rankine of Adamhill,

O Rough, rude, ready-witted Rankine,
The wale o cocks for fun and drinkin!
There's mony godly folks are thinkin
Your dreams an tricks
Will send you, Korah-like a sinkin,
Straught to auld Nick's.

Epistle to John Rankine, 1784

and John Wilson, a schoolmaster, session clerk, grocer and amateur doctor specialising in quack remedies who was the subject of Burns's lampoon, *Death and Dr. Hornbook* in 1785.

With these and others, including Gilbert, Robert was a founder member, later to become President, of the Tarbolton Bachelors' Club; formed to debate matters of love, education and social standing. There would be no "swearing and profane language" and no more than sixteen bachelors in number who would have a "frank, honest and open heart" and each "just as happy

John Wilson

as this world can make him." Doubtless some drink would also have been taken.

In keeping with his expanding social circle, Burns found himself involved in his first serious romance and his first real stab at letterwriting. Burns sent letters to Elizabeth Gebbie, a servant girl from Galston; his advances, written in stuffy, formal and rather self-conscious manner. Three of Robert's songs of this time refer to her — *Farewell to Eliza*, *The Lass of Cessnock Bank* and the one containing the classic second verse, *Mary Morison*.

Yestreen, when to the trembling string
The dance gaed thro' the lighted ha
To thee my fancy took its wing,
I sat but neither heard nor saw;
Tho this was fair, and that was braw,
And yon the toast of a' the town,
I sighed and said among them a',
'Ye are na Mary Morison!'.

Mary Morison, 1780

Burns became a Freemason in 1781, at St. David Lodge in Tarbolton. Through this he made many influential friends, including the lawyer Gavin Hamilton, Dr. John MacKenzie, and James Dalrymple who was to introduce Burns to the Earl of Glencairn.

Within this dear Mansion may wayward contortion
Or withered Envy ne'er enter;
May secrecy round be the mystical bound,
And brotherly Love be the centre!

Ye Sons of old Killie— a Masonic Song, 1786

Meanwhile Robert and Gilbert experimented with flax growing at Lochlea with some measure of success, Robert receiving a subsidy of £3 in 1783. If he could "dress" the flax and thus prepare it for the spinners, it could have proved profitable. With this end in view Robert travelled to Irvine in the summer of 1781 where he entered into partnership with a flax-dresser, perhaps in the High Street. The attempt was a failure, the shop eventually burned down and Burns, already ill and deeply depressed, wrote to his father of the "... weakness of my nerves..." and a wish that "...perhaps very soon, I shall bid an eternal adieu to all the pains... of weary life...". He later wrote

of a "hypochondriac complaint," which was in fact the beginnings of endocarditis, brought on by the overwork and poor diet of the years at Mount Oliphant.

He made one particular friend in Irvine, a sailor, Richard Brown, whom Burns held in high esteem; Robert claiming Brown taught him the art of seduction. Brown did, however, encourage him to publish his poetry. It is not clear why, but Burns stayed on in Irvine until the spring of 1782, and seemed to have enjoyed the colour and specta- cle of a busy port.

"Observations, Hints, Songs, Scraps of Poetry &c. by Robt Burnes; a man who had little art in making money, and still less in keeping it; but was, however, a man of some sense, a great deal of honesty, and unbounded good-will to every

creature rational and irrational. — As he was but little indebted to scholastic education, and bred at a plough-tail,..."

Thus began Burns' *First Commonplace Book* and with it the myth of the "untutored ploughman" which Burns used to his advantage.Though surely the man who learnt his "tuneful trade from every bough" was almost certainly the first to find knowledge of the great English poets, the old Scots Makars of the 15th and 16th centuries, English grammar, some French grammar and a little Latin falling

from the trees as he stood at the plough.

The simple Bard, rough at the rustic plough,
Learning his tuneful trade from every bough;
                              The Brigs of Ayr, 1786

My talents they were not the worst; Nor yet my education O;
Resolv'd was I, at least to try, To mend my situation O.
                              My Father was a Farmer, 1782

All hail! my own inspired Bard!
In me thy native Muse regard!
Nor longer mourn thy fate is hard,
Thus poorly low!
I come to give thee such reward,
As we bestow.

The Vision, 1786

If miry ridges and dirty dunghills
are to engross... my soul immortal,
I had better been a rook or
a magpie at once.

Letter to Mrs Dunlop, 1789

    While Burns began his *First Common-place Book*, home matters were worsening. Due to lack of a written agreement, William Burnes and McLure were in dispute, McLure eventually taking out a writ of sequestration, William countering with a petition to the Court of Session in Edinburgh. By this time, however, William's health was so poor that Robert and Gil-

Gavin Hamilton

1751 -1805

bert had to face the fact that they would have to consider the future without their father. This is where the Mauchline lawyer Gavin Hamilton entered the Burns story. On hearing of the family circumstances he offered them the lease of Mossgiel Farm for £90 a year, should William die, and they be "driven forth... forlorn."

I readily and freely grant,

He downa see a poor man want;

What's no his ain, he winna tak it,

What ance he says, he winna break it;

A Dedication to Gavin Hamilton Esq, 1786

A girl called Elizabeth Paton with whom Burns had a brief affair, was by now helping Agnes around the house. This culminated later with what seemed to recur after all such of Robert's amours

— a pregnancy. Burns wrote a bawdy verse concerning his interest in her, entering it in his Commonplace Book. *My Girl she's Airy.*

His interest did not go unnoticed and served to sow further seeds of doubt in his dying father's mind about leaving the family's future in his hands. On 27 January 1784, news came that William had won his case against David McLure. However, the suit had used up all his of savings as well as his strength and the family physician, Dr. John Mackenzie warned them to expect the worst.

On 13 February, while Robert and his sister, Isabella, kept watch over their father, William called his daughter to him, telling her to follow the path of virtue and suchlike, adding that there was one about whom he had misgivings, Robert asked: "Father, is it me you mean?" to which he replied that it was. Distraught, Robert turned away, the tears running down his cheeks. A few hours later his father

27

died. So with an unfeeling parting shot, the man who had given the poet life and by forcing too much hardship on him at a tender age was unwittingly to take it away, passed on.

O ye, whose cheek the tear of pity stains,
Draw near with pious rev'rence and attend!
Here lie the loving husband's dear remains,
The tender father, and the gen'rous friend.

The pitying heart that felt for human woe;
The dauntless heart that fear'd no human pride;
The friend of man, to vice alone a foe;
For ev'n his failings lean'd to virtue's side.

Epitaph on my Father

The move to Mossgiel took place in March 1784 and as the head of the family, Robert was full of resolve — "I entered upon this farm with a full resolution, 'Come, go to, I will be wise' — I read farming books; I calculated crops, I attended markets; and in short, in spite of 'The devil, the world and the flesh,' I believe I would have been a wise man; but the first year from unfortunately buying in bad seed, the second from a late harvest... and I returned 'Like the dog to his vomit, and the sow that was washed to her wallowing in the mire."

Gilbert described the farm as "mostly on a cold wet bottom". It was to prove little better than the farms at Mount Oliphant or Lochlie. As the tenant, Robert could, according to the local custom, be known by the property, and did so in *O leave Novels.*

Mossgiel

O leave novels, ye Mauchline belles —
Ye're safer at your spinning wheel!
Such witching books are baited hooks
For rakish rooks like Rob Mossgiel.

O leave Novels, 1784

Mossgiel lies in the parish of Mauchline and it was here that Burns made new social acquaintances. Along with John Richmond and James Smith, Burns witnessed the scenes which inspired *The Jolly Beggars* in Poosie Nansie's Tavern where a collection of miserable beggars drink and make merry. The biographers

Henley and Henderson described it as "Humanity caught in the act". Burns himself, however, thought poorly of the poem and only liked the verse:

A fig for those by law protected!
Liberty's a glorious feast!
Courts for cowards were erected,
Churches built to please the priest!

The years from 1784 to 1786 were to prove fruitful for his muse and equally busy in affairs of the heart. Besides this, from the summer of 1784 until June 1785, Gavin Hamilton was in dispute with the Kirk Session. William Fisher, a narrow, orthodox elder, had singled out Hamilton for unnecessary absence; setting out on a journey on the Sabbath; neglect of family worship and abusive letters to the Kirk Session. On appeal to the Presbytery of Ayr, they found in Hamilton's favour and likewise a counter appeal to the synod of Ayr and Glasgow was for Hamilton, a victory celebrated by Burns in one of the finest satires ever penned — *Holy Willie's Prayer.*

O Thou that in the Heavens does dwell,
Wha, as it pleases best Thysel,
Sends ane to Heaven, an ten to Hell
A' for thy Glory,
And no for onie guid or ill
They've done before thee!

Lord, mind Gau'n Hamilton's deserts:
He drinks, an swears, an plays at cartes,
Yet has sae monie takin arts,
Wi great and sma'
Frae God's ain Priest the people's hearts,
He steals awa.

Holy Willie's Prayer, 1785

It is generally thought that Burns first met Jean Armour in 1785. She was the daughter of James Armour, a master stonemason in Mauchline and almost 19 when they first met. Although the relationship was slow to begin with, it grew after Elizabeth Paton gave birth to Elizabeth, "Dear-bought Bess",

on 22 May 1785. The outcome, almost inevitably, was that by the end of the year, Burns had made Jean pregnant. Burns declared his intention of marrying her in a written document, binding by Scots law, as was the fact that they were married by "use and wont". Her father mutilated the paper, and Jean was sent to Paisley. Thus began, rather unpromisingly, the relationship which would end only with the poet's death some 11 years later.

Miss Miller is fine, Miss Markland's divine,
Miss Smith she has wit, and Miss Betty is braw:
There's beauty and fortune to get wi Miss Morton,
But Armour's the jewel for me o' them a'.

The Belles of Mauchline, 1784

Burns, his pride dented, reacted in

melodramatic fashion to what he saw as Jean's desertion of him, as he wrote to Gavin Hamilton on 15 April — "Perdition seize her falsehood and perjurious perfidy!... She is ill  advised". To add to this, he had become involved with another girl, Margaret Campbell, of whom more later, and was applying for a Bachelor's Certificate from his minister "Daddy" Auld. His cure for these ills was emigration, as he wrote to John Arnot "Already the holy beagles, the houghmagandie pack, begin to snuff the scent, & I expect every moment to see them cast off, and hear them after me in full cry: but as I am an old fox, I shall give them dodging & doubling for it: & by and bye, I intend to earth among the mountains of Jamaica".It would seem to have been more than a dramatic gesture, as he made concrete plans to sail on the *Nancy* from Greenock.

He saw Misfortune's cauld nor-west
Langs mustering up a bitter blast;
A jillet brak his heart at last—
Ill may she be!
So took a berth afore the mast
An' owre the sea.

On a Scotch Bard, gone to the West Indies, 1786

When Jean returned in June, Burns, although still planning to emigrate, told David Brice, a shoemaker in Glasgow "I do still love her to distraction..." Jean sent a confession to the minister, naming Robert as the father, whereupon they were required to submit three times to public rebuke in the Kirk. Auld allowed the poet to stand in his pew, refusing Jean's pleas to have him beside her in the place of repentance "which bred a great trouble". As a consequence, Burns

gained his Bachelor's Certificate. His anxieties were not entirely eased as Margaret Campbell prepared for marriage in Campbeltown.

A fornicator — loun he call'd me,

An said my faut frae bliss expell'd me;

I own'd the tale was true he tell'd me,

'But, what the matter?'

Quo' I 'I fear unless ye geld me,

I'll ne'er be better'

To a Tailor, 1786

Margaret Campbell was born near Dunoon in 1766 and was employed for a time by Gavin Hamilton as a nursemaid. Exactly where and when she met Robert Burns is not known but it appears to have been soon after Jean's 'desertion'. They parted company on May 14, 1786. Burns gave her his two-volume pocket Bible as a parting gift, inscribed "...Robert Burns, Mossgavill." He made no declaration of marriage to her. She returned to her parents' home. In October she crossed to Greenock, possibly and very probably, pregnant. According to Burns, she was on her way to meet him. At any rate Margaret died, perhaps in childbirth and was buried in the old West Highland kirkyard. Mary's parents destroyed all correspondence from Burns and forbade mention of his name.

Apart from a couple of indifferent poems, Burns kept the lid firmly closed on the affair, thus leaving Margaret Campbell to become "Highland Mary", Robert's only real love, according to 19th-century romanticists who saw her as his "virgin bride of fancy". When James Armour learnt of Burns' defection plans, he had Jean sign a complaint against him. The outcome was a writ against Robert. Burns took swift action by conveying all his property and any profits from his projected publications of poems to his brother Gilbert, and went into hiding at Allan's farm at Old Rome Foord, near Irvine — "I am wandering from one friend's house to another, and like a true son of the Gospel, 'have nowhere to lay my head' ."

Meanwhile, Robert's writing had been prolific during 1784-86 and he had approached John Wilson, a Kilmarnock printer, with a view to publishing. The result of this would of course alter everything, carrying Robert's fame to a national (and ultimately international) level and, of course, the sniff of money would soften James Armour's attitude completely.

Some rhyme a neebor's name to lash;

Some rhyme (vain thought) for needfu cash;

Some rhyme to court the countra clash,

An raise a din;

For me, an aim I never fash;

I rhyme for fun.

To James Smith

On 31 July 1786, *Poems, Chiefly in the Scottish Dialect* was published. Robert pressed on with his Jamai-

Gilbert Burns

1760 -1827

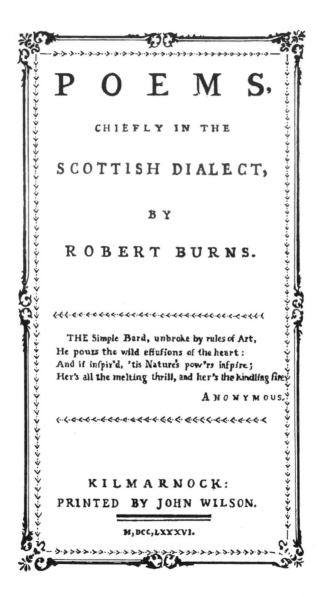

POEMS,

CHIEFLY IN THE

SCOTTISH DIALECT,

BY

ROBERT BURNS.

THE Simple Bard, unbroke by rules of Art,
He pours the wild effusions of the heart:
And if infpir'd, 'tis Nature's pow'rs infpire;
Her's all the melting thrill, and her's the kindling fire.

ANONYMOUS.

KILMARNOCK:
PRINTED BY JOHN WILSON.

M,DCC,LXXXVI.

can plans and paid farewell visits to Tarbolton Lodge and to various friends around the county. He set off for Greenock, stopping off at the house of the Rev. George Lawrie, minister of Loudon who felt that Burns should not leave Scotland and Robert let the *Nancy* sail without him, planning to set out later on the *Bell*. On 3 September Jean delivered twins, naming them Robert and Jean.

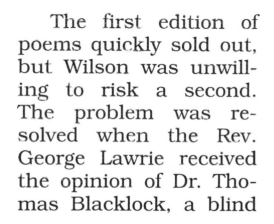

Wish me luck dear Richmond!

Armour has just brought me a fine boy and girl at one throw.

God bless the little dears!

Letter to John Richmond

Rev. George Lawrie

1727 -99

The first edition of poems quickly sold out, but Wilson was unwilling to risk a second. The problem was resolved when the Rev. George Lawrie received the opinion of Dr. Thomas Blacklock, a blind minister and minor poet in Edinburgh, and this had the effect of Burns also allowing the *Bell* to sail without him and seeking a second edition in Scotland's capital. On 15 November he wrote to Mrs Dunlop stating that "I am thinking to go to Edinburgh in a week or two at farthest, to throw off a second impression of my book..."

On reading the Kilmarnock volume, Mrs Frances Dunlop of Dunlop was roused from her state of mourning, having recently lost her husband. She was best pleased with *The Cotter's Saturday Night* and she began a correspondence with the poet of which 79 letters survive. She became his confidante and something of a mother-confessor. Mrs Dunlop sent off a letter to Mossgiel for six copies; Burns could only supply five and sent this comment. "I am fully persuaded that there is not any class of Mankind so feeling alive to the titillations of applause as the sons of Parnassus, nor is it easy to conceive how the heart of the poor bard dances with rapture, when those, whose character in life gives them a right to be polite Judges, honour him with their approbation".

Since then, my honour'd, first of friends,
On this poor being all depends
Let us th' important Now employ
And live as those that never die.

To Mrs Dunlop, 1790

Dr. Thomas Blacklock
1721 -94

Doctor Blacklock's verdict was, "There is a pathos and delicacy in his serious poems; a vein of wit and humour in those of a more festive turn, which cannot be too much admired, nor too warmly approved ... It were therefore much to be wished ... that a second edition ... could immediately be printed." He added that it could have "more universal circulation than any thing of the kind which has been published within my memory". In the preface to the Kilmarnock edition, Burns put forward the notion of himself as an untutored ploughman and unacquainted with the "requisites for commending Poet by rule", a ruse which fascinated genteel Edinburgh society. Henry Mackenzie, attorney and novelist, waxed lyrical "... this Heaven-taught ploughman, from his humble and unlettered station, has looked upon men and manners". John Logan, however, spotted the fact that Burns was "as well acquainted with the English poets as I was".

Thus on 27 November, Burns, on a "pownie" borrowed from George Reid, set out to conquer Edinburgh. The journey to Edinburgh took two days, Burns spending one night with friends near Biggar in Lanarkshire. In the capital he was met by his old friend John Richmond, now a clerk in a law office and with whom Robert would lodge in Baxter's Close, a narrow wynd with high buildings on either side. Here servants emptied the contents of chamber pots and all manner of refuse into the streets below, described by James Boswell in 1773 as "a good deal odoriferous".

Burns wrote *Edina, Scotia's darling seat* soon after his arrival, and met such luminaries as Lord Glencairn, Henry Erskine and the fourth Duke of Gordon. "I am in a fair way of becoming as eminent as Thomas à Kempis, or John Bunyan; and you may expect henceforth to see my birthday inserted among the wonderful events..." he wrote to Gavin Hamilton. He very quickly made influential friends, arranged a second edition and gained the subscriptions of the Caledonian Hunt, some

Edina!
Scotia's darling seat,
All hail thy palaces and tow'rs.

I shelter in thy
honour'd shade.
        Address to Edinburgh.
        1786

46

of Edinburgh's wealthy elite.

Robert Burns first met James Cunningham, 14th Earl of Glencairn in 1785, when the Earl backed an "Auld Licht" (Orthodox Calvinist) candidate for Kilmarnock Parish whom Burns lampooned in *The Ordination*, winning Glencairn's admiration. Glencairn welcomed the poet warmly, taking 24 copies of the second edition and used his influence in the Caledonian Hunt, which took up a further 100. He was to remain a close friend and ally to Burns until his untimely death in 1791.

The mother may forget the child
That smiles sae sweetly on her knee;
But I' ll remember thee Glencairn,
And a' that thou hast done for me!

Lament for the Earl of Glencairn, 1791

Burns, writing to John Ballantine, an Ayr banker, reported "my avowed patrons and patronesses are the Duchess of Gordon, the Countess of Glencairn, with my lord and lady Betty, the Dean of Faculty, Sir John Whitefoord". Soon he became acquainted with anyone of social standing in the capital worth knowing and for a time no social gathering of "the noblesse" was complete without the "Rustic Bard".

It was not a complete victory however for he had suffered a bout of illness on arrival in the city and less than two months later, writing to the Rev. William Greenfield "Never did Saul's

48

armour sit so heavy on David when going to encounter Goliah, as does the encumbering robe of public notice... some 'names dear to fame' have invested me... I am afraid, I shall have bitter reason to repent".

Thy Sons, Edina, social, kind.

With open arms the stranger hail;

Address to Edinburgh, 1786

Although Burns enjoyed the patronage of the select Edinburgh crowd, he was not entirely comfortable with them. He was the latest fad and he charmed them with  his outstanding and often astonishing personality to

Dugald Stewart

which many of them later testified. Testimonies to the poet's character whilst in Edinburgh are a valuable insight as to the special charms he exhibited. Dugald Stewart, (1753-1828), Professor of Moral Philosophy at Edinburgh University, in a letter to the "Younger" recalled — "His manners were then, as they continued ever afterwards, simple, manly, and independent; strongly expressive of conscious genius and worth; but without... forwardness, arrogance, or vanity... Nothing, perhaps, was more remarkable among his various attainments, than the fluency, and precision, and originality of his language, when he spoke in company..."

Walter Scott, then aged 15, met Burns at Professor Ferguson's — "His person was strong and robust, his manners rustic, not clownish;... I think his countenance was more massive than it looks... in the portraits... The eye alone, I think, indicated the poetical character and temperament. It... glowed (I say literally glowed) when he spoke with feeling or interest. I never saw such another eye in a human head..." In spite of the glowing references, Burns sought company more congenial to his own particular whims, which Edinburgh could supply in abundance. The club which Burns found most conducive was the

Walter Scott

Crochallan Fencibles. Two of the members, William Smellie and Robert Cleghorn, would receive items of the bard's bawdy verse, later published as *The Merry Muses of Caledonia*. One of the poems which appeared for the first time in the Edinburgh edition was *Address to a Haggis* now famous at Burns Suppers, but written while at a meeting of the Crochallan Fencibles, apparently more as a satire than a salute.

Fair fa' your honest, sonsie face,

Great chieftan o' the puddin' - race

Aboon them a' ye tak your place,

Puinch, tripe, or thairm:

Weel are ye wordy of a grace

As long's my airm.

Address to a Haggis, 1786

The second edition was quickly exhausted, the type reset hastily, and a third, riddled with errors was issued. Creech bought the copyright from Burns for 100 guineas, although technically, he bought nothing, Gilbert Burns being the true holder. Creech withheld final settlement until 1789 with Burns receiving around £853 after costs.

Robert Ainslie
1766 - 1838

To Mrs Dunlop, Burns wrote that he wished "to make leisurely pilgrimages through Caledonia;" and thus, in the company of a young law student, Robert Ainslie, set out to tour the Borders. He made his first crossing to English soil at Coldstream, visited Roxburgh, Jedburgh, Kelso, Selkirk and viewed a farm at Dalswinton near Dumfries which Patrick Miller had offered him, though he was unimpressed. He became a Freeman of Dumfries and an honorary archmason at Eyemouth to add to his honour from the Grand Lodge of Scotland. On 10 May he visited Wauchope House, and left these lines:

The Bridge over the Tweed at Coldstream

Ee'n then a wish (I mind its pow'r) —
A wish that to my latest hour
Shall strongly heave my breast:
That I for poor auld Scotland's sake
Some useful plan or book could make
Or sing a sang at least...

To the Guid-wife of Wauchope House, 1787

At Dumfries, Burns received a letter from Edinburgh informing him that May Cameron, a servant girl was pregnant, his reply "...give her ten or twelve shillings... and advise her out to some country friends" was ignored by her and she would not be bought off. Robert returned to Mossgiel to find where he had once been treated with suspicion, he was now

Linlithgow Palace

regarded with some reverence, the Armours now warmly welcoming to him. His major concern was how to make a living.

For care and trouble set your thought,

Ev'n when your end's attained;

And a' your views may come to naught

Where every nerve is strained.

Epistle to a Young Friend, 1786

"I write this on my tour through a country where savage streams tumble over savage mountains, thinly overspread with savage flocks which starvingly support as savage inhabitants".

In June Burns had set off on a short Highland tour, through west Argyll. He kept no journal and returned to Mossgiel where on 2 August 1787 he wrote what is now known as the "autobiographical letter" to Dr John Moore. He returned to Edinburgh and with William Nicol set out on another Highland tour. At Linlithgow, he showed himself to be no narrow "Holy Willie" Calvinist. "What a poor, pimping business is a Presbyterian place of worship, dirty, narrow and squalid, stuck in a corner of old Popish grandeur such as Linlithgow and, much more, Melrose! ceremony and show, if judiciously thrown in, absolutely necessary for the bulk of mankind both in religious and civil matters".

John Murry, 4th
Duke of Atholl
1755 - 1830

Whilst on tour the poet visited Bannockburn, and when at Stirling he gave vent to his Jacobite sympathies by engraving on a tavern window with a diamond ring:

The injured Stewart line is gone,
A race outlandish fills their throne;
An idiot race, to honour lost;
Who know them best despise them most.

On Stirling, 1787

From Stirling, he and Nicol went through Harvieston, Crieff, Taymouth,

Aberfeldy and on to Blair Atholl, where they dined with the Duke, and met, for the first time, Graham of Fintry. After crossing Culloden Moor, Burns was warmly welcomed by the Duke and Duchess of Gordon who asked him to stay overnight. Nicol, offended at not being included, insisted that they both move on. They travelled on to Aberdeen and thence to the home of his paternal ancestors, writing to Gilbert on 17 September. "I spent two days among our relations, and found our aunts, Jean and Isabel still alive and hale old woman". From there, they travelled back to Edinburgh to deal with Creech's delays and consult with Patrick Miller over his farm at Dalswinton.

In October 1787 Burns embarked on a fourth tour, this time along the Ochil hills. This time his companion was Dr James Adair, a relative of Mrs Dunlop. He went

Margaret Chalmers 1763 - 1843

through Linlithgow to Stirling to join Nicol. At Harvieston House he met Margaret Chalmers, who made a deep impression on him. She was the nearest to an intellectual equal of all the women he wooed and he appears to have hoped for marriage but she was already engaged to an Edinburgh advocate. When he wrote his final letter to her, in September 1788, pondering on the fact that he may never see her again, he said "...I could sit down and cry like a child!"

On 20 October they returned to Edinburgh.

My Peggy's face, my Peggy's form,
The frost of hermit Age might warm;
My Peggy's worth, my Peggy's mind
Might charm the first of human kind

My Peggys' Face, 1787

While considering his future and attempting to settle with Creech, Burns was not idle; he began collecting and improving Scots songs for James Johnson.

In his second winter in Edinburgh, the

Example of Burns' musical notation from a letter to George Thomson, November 8, 1792

poet was forced, through Creech's refusal to settle, to linger for many weeks in the capital. He had a further bout of illness and mourned the death of Jean, one of the twins in September. For the moment, he channelled his energies into Scots songs, writing to Richmond, on 25 October "I am busy at present assisting with a Collection of Scotch Songs... — It is to contain all the Scotch Songs, those that have already been set to music and those that have not, that can be found..."

Contented wi' little, and cantie wi' mair,

Whene'er I foregather wi sorrow and care,

I gie them a skelp, as they're creepin' alang,

Wi a cog o gude swats, and an auld Scottish sang.

Contented wi Little, 1794

58

On 6 December 1787, Burns attended a tea-party where he was introduced to Mrs McLehose. She was 29 years old, a mother of three children and was estranged from James McLehose, who was in Jamaica. Burns and Nancy began meeting for tea and communicating by letter. The poet was certainly smitten with her, and it would seem, she with him, but his usual ardour was dashed on the rocks of her religious fervour. In their letters to each other he became "Sylvander" and she "Clarinda".

It appears to have been a battle of wills, his for intimacy, her's to keep him at arm's length.

Fair Empress of the Poet's soul,
And Queen of Poetesses;
Clarinda, take this little boon,
This humble pair of glasses.
　　　Verses to Clarinda (with a present
　　　　of a pair of drinking glasses)

On 18 February, Burns left Edinburgh, spending an evening in Glasgow, another in Paisley and two days at Dunlop House with Mrs Dunlop before arriving at Mossgiel. From here he wrote to Agnes McLehose, claiming to have finished with Jean Armour — "to compare her with my Clarinda; 'twas setting the expiring glimmer of a farthing taper beside the cloudless glory of the meridian sun". If "Clarinda" believed the poet to be serious in the matter of Jean, his future actions would prove otherwise.

He had already written to Glencairn, and to Graham of Fintry urging them to use their influence to gain him a position in the Excise. Jean had by now given birth once more to twins, fated to die within a few days.

Will generous Graham list to his Poet's wail?
(It soothes poor Misery, heark'ning to her tale)
And hear him curse the light he first survey'd,
And doubly curse the luckless rhyming trade?
To Robert Graham, Esq. of Fintry, 1791

Punch bowl, a wedding gift from James Armour

In April Burns wrote to James Smith, stating that he has "lately and privately given a matrimonial title to my corpus" and to Mrs Dunlop, "Her happiness or misery was in my hands, and who could trifle with such a deposit". The exact details of the marriage are shrouded in mystery, but the parish register for 5 August 1788 states that "Compeared Robert Burns with Jean Armour, his alleged spouse", that they "both acknowledged their irregular marriage"... to "adhere faithfully to one another as husband and wife". It was signed by William Auld, Robert Burns, and Jean Armour, (in the poet's handwriting) with Burns obliged

The house in Mauchline where Robert and Jean lived between their marriage and Ellisland

to give a guinea "for behoof of the poor". He did not inform Agnes McLehose, she hearing of it later, perhaps from Ainslie.

She is a winsome wee thing,
She is a handsome wee thing,
She is a lo'some wee thing,
This sweet wee wife o' mine.
The warld's wrack we share o't,
The warstle and care o't,
Wi her I'll blythely bear it,
And think my lot divine.

My Wife's a winsome wee thing, 1792

Burns took tenancy of Ellisland, on the banks of the Nith, near Dumfries, in June 1788. The farm was unfenced, the soil extremely poor and was perhaps even worse than any which the poet's father had managed. It did not even have a farmhouse, and Burns, having just completed six weeks of Excise instruction at Mauchline, left Jean and the children at Mossgiel until a farmhouse could be built. For his part, Robert stayed in a cold damp hut on the farm, a condition which must have further damaged his health. In spite of the spartan conditions, he still managed to pen some humorous verse:

Here, for my wanted, rhyming raptures,
I sit and count my sins by chapters;
For life and spunk like ither Christians,
I'm dwindled down to mere existence;

Wi' a' this care and a' this grief,
And sma' sma' prospect of relief,
And nought but peat reek i' my head,
How can I write what ye can read?

Epistle to Hugh Parker, 1788

In spite of the massive labours Ellis-land demanded, Burns set about the business in high spirits. If all else failed, there was always an excise post to fall back on. He began the enterprise with a run of ill health, but his marriage and strong family instinct seems to have pulled him through. Progress on the building was slow, the poet writing to Thomas Boyd, "For G-d's sake let me but within the shell of it". Eventually Burns was able to move into one end while the other was completed, "before it be plaistered". While still living in the hut and wishing the house was finished with both him and Jean in it, he wrote one of his most tender love songs.

Of a' the airts the wind can blaw,
I dearly like the west,
For there the bonie lassie lives,
The lassie I lo' e best:
There's wild woods grow, and rivers row,
And monie a hill between;
But day and night my fancy's flight
Is ever wi' my Jean.

Of a' the airts, 1788

In September, Burns wrote to Graham of Fintry, explaining that the farm was proving less than profitable, and due to financial help given to Gilbert at Moss-giel, he had no cash to make

up the shortfall. He proposed a way to gain a post in the Excise, which he regarded as his "sheet anchor in life". Noting that the local excise officer was "owing to some legacies... quite opulent" and "a removal could do him no injury" he would be willing to take over next summer. A few weeks later, Robert thought better of it — "I could not bear to injure a poor fellow by ousting him to make way for myself".

Searching auld wives' barrels,

Ochon, the day

That clarty barm should stain my laurels!

But what'll ye say?

These movin things ca'd wives an' weans

Wad move the very hearts o stanes.

Extemporaneous Effusion;

on being appointed to the Excise, 1789

By this time Robert and Jean had under their care the children of his uncle, Robert Burnes, who had died. There was also the poet's brother William, who, unable to settle to any occupation was boarding at Ellisland. Later, after finding work in Newcastle he went to London, where he died in 1790.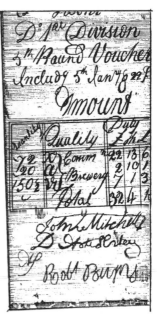

A year after his request to Graham, the poet's wish was granted, and on 27 October 1789 he was sworn in as an Excise officer in the Dumfries First Itinerancy. This involved a ride of 200 miles a week on his own horse, and updating his books at night. He received £50 per year plus half of the fines and half the goods seized. He did this while still attempting to make Ellisland workable.

The De'il cam fiddlin thro' the town,
And danced awa' wi th' Exciseman;
And ilka wife cried 'Auld Mahoun,
We wish you luck o' the prize man'

On the list of excise officers, next to

Dr Hugh Blair

Henry Mackenzie

Dr Thomas Blacklock

"Even in Scotland, the provincial dialect... is now read with a difficulty which greatly damps the pleasure of the reader... as nearly to destroy the pleasure".
Henry Mackenzie, 1786

Dugald Stewart

Dr John Moore

the poet's name was the comment 'Never tryed — a Poet'. Later it was added — 'Turns out well'. He was to prove an efficient officer.

In January 1789, Burns wrote that he had "...a hundred different Poetic plans, pastoral, georgic, dramatic etc..." He was beginning to fall prey to the urgings of his Edinburgh following who wished him to avoid "the peculiarities of Scottish phraseology" and instead employ a more high-flowing augustan English. When Burns did so, on occasion, he met with less success, although much of his poetry did already contain verses in standard English, sometimes shifting somewhat awkwardly between the two. The overwork was taking its toll on Robert's health, he had an attack of "malignant squinancy and low fever" and by Christmas he was "groaning under the miseries of a diseased nervous system". Burns, in spite of his health, still wrote and made new friendships.

Robert Riddell of Glenriddell, who lived close to Ellisland, was recruited as an antiquarian to supply information on Nithsdale for Camden's *Britannia* and was an amateur musician. He gave Burns a key to a gazebo at Friars' Carse to ena-

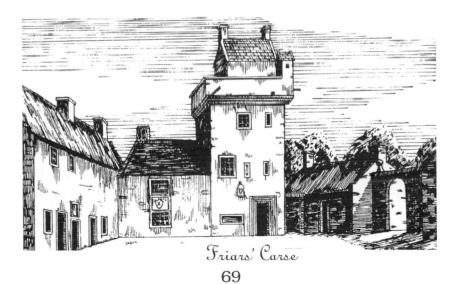

Friars' Carse

ble him to write and welcomed him as a friend.

In the summer of 1789, Burns met Captain Francis Grose who had published his *Antiquities of England and Wales*, with 589 drawings of his own, and now set out to do the same for Scotland. Burns suggested that Grose should include Alloway Kirk in his book, to which he agreed on condition that Robert provide him with a "witch story".

Hear, Land o Cakes, and brither Scots,

Frae Maidenkirk to Johnie Groat's; ——

If there's a hole in a' your coats,

I rede you tent it:

A chield's amang you taking notes,

And, faith, he'll prent it.

On the late Captain Grose's
peregrinations thro' Scotland, 1790

The "witch story" which Burns provided was perhaps his most famous poem, and indeed his last great piece of original verse, *Tam O' Shanter*. Burns based it on a folk story concerning Alloway Kirk which was "an awful warning to the Carrick farmers, not to stay too late in Ayr markets". However once in the poet's hands, the tale became a fast moving narrative with Burns occasionally dropping in personal observation. Burns begins *Tam O' Shanter* by setting the scene of the end of a busy market day in Ayr, with people making their way home while

...we sit bousing at the nappy,

An getting fou and unco happy,...

While Tam's wife, Kate, sits at home —

Gathering her brows like gathering storm,
Nursing her wrath to keep it warm

Having painted the picture, Burns tells the story beginning with Tam's drinking partner, Souter Johnny

The Souter tauld his queerest stories:
The landlord's laugh was ready chorus:

The poem is remarkable for its rhythm and swift changes of pace, as Tam rides home on his "grey meare Meg" heading towards Alloway Kirk, passing the sites of various grisly murders and local superstitions until he reaches the Kirk to see it brightly lit.

When glimmering thro the groaning trees
Kirk-Alloway seem'd in a bleeze.

In the church he sees "auld Nick, in the shape o' beast" playing the pipes, as the ghosts perform "hornpipes, jigs, strathspeys and reels", while on the "haly table" were displayed objects which "even to name wad be unlawfu".

One of the dancers was "ae winsome wench" wearing a short chemise, and Tam, losing all reason, shouts —

Weel done, Cutty sark!
And in an instant all was dark!

The ghosts give Tam chase and as he reaches the "key-stane o' the brig", the young spirit grabs the horse's tail and "left poor Maggie scarce a stump".

And so the poem finishes with a warning.

Whene'er to drink you are inclin'd,

Or cutty sarks run in your mind,

Think! ye may buy the joys o'er dear',

Remember Tam O' Shanter's mare.

Tam O' Shanter, 1790

Burns is popularly but erroneously believed to have written *Tam O' Shanter* in a day, and he felt that it "showed a finishing polish" which he despaired of "ever excelling". It is perhaps his best known work and first appeared in *The Edinburgh Magazine* in March 1791 and then in Grose's *Antiquities of Scotland* for which it was written.

In spite of holding down the excise post and farming Ellisland, Robert still partook in the social life of Dumfries. He became "treasurer, librarian and censor" to the Monkland Friendly Society which was to provide its members with literary classics; he was also on the free list of the Dumfries Theatre Royal. For the latter he hoped to write plays, although in fact, he provided only a few prologues. He also became involved in local politics, to the extent of writing Election Ballads in 1790 — *The Fête Champetre*, *The Five Carlins*, *Election Ballad for Westerha*, and *Second Epistle to Robert Giulium* which now are a little obscure, due to their dimmed local significance.

To thee, lov'd Nith, thy gladsome plains,
Where late wi careless thought I rang'd
Though prest wi care and sunk in woe,
To thee I bring a heart unchang'd.

The Banks of Nith, 1789

Dumfries c1800

The poet's political life became more apparent when he wrote to the *Edinburgh Evening Courant* in defence of the Stuart dynasty after Joseph Kirkpatrick, the minister of Dunscore denounced them from the pulpit. In the letter he said "The Stuarts have been condemned... for the folly... of their attempts in 1715 and 1745. That they failed, I bless my God..., but cannot join in the ridicule against them..." He would later have more to say regarding the House of Stuart and gave vent to Jacobite sympathies in verse on many occasions.

Here's a health to them that's awa',
Here's a health to them that's awa;
Here's a health to Charlie, the chief o' the clan
Altho that his band be but sma'
May Liberty meet wi success!
May prudence protect her frae evil!
May tyrants and tyranny tine i' the mist,
And wander their way to the Devil!

Here's a Health, 1792

In September 1790 Burns had spoken of giving up, or "subletting" Ellisland. It was in fact, the following summer before Patrick Miller sold the farm and Robert was able to sell his standing crops and farm gear. Ill health once more dogged the poet and his arm was broken in a fall in March and when he returned from Gilbert's wedding in August, he injured his leg. Burns and family moved into a house in what is now Bank Street in Dumfries. Added to young Robert, Francis and William Nicol was the child to whom Ann Park, a barmaid at the Globe Tavern, had given birth. In Dumfries, the poet quickly gained friends and admirers, notably William Maxwell, a doctor trained in France who had seen service in the French Revolution as a Republican and John Syme who became Distributor of Stamps, whose office was below Burns' first home in the town.

No more of your guests, be they titled or not,

And cookery the first in the nation;

Who is proof to thy personal converse and wit,

Is proof to all other temptation.

Extempore to Mr Syme, 1795

Other friends included the Rev. James Gray, who recalled the care Burns took over his children's education; Thomas White, a Latin master; the farmer John Clark, Robert Cleghorn and Peter Hill, a bookseller. Robert also made firm friends with his superiors in the Excise. His district supervisor Alexander Findlater, who took the poet to task over a discrepancy in one of his entries, for which Burns was blameless "...I shall be peculiarly unfortunate if my character shall fall a sacrifice to the dark manoeuvres of a smuggler". The smuggler was William Lorimer of

Cairnhill near Penpont — but not his namesake from Kenny's Hall, whose daughter Jean, Burns had a fancy for. It was perhaps because of her somewhat unpoetic surname that Burns christened her "Chloris".

Ah, Chloris, since it may not be,
That thou of love wilt hear;
If from the lover thou maun flee,
Yet let the friend be dear.

Ah, Chloris, 1793

Jean Lorimer 'Chloris' 1775 -1831

Another of his excise superiors, John Mitchell was a friend; indeed at one of Collector Mitchell's Excise Court dinners, Burns composed the famous song.

The Deil's awa', the Deil's awa',
The Deil's awa' wi th' Exciseman'
He's danc'd awa, he's danc'd awa,
He's danc'd awa wi' the Exciseman.

The Deil's awa' wi' the Exciseman

By far the most important of all the poet's women friends was Maria Riddell. Born in London, nee Woodley, she published her experiences of life in the West Indies in 1792, where her father was Captain General of the Lee-

Maria Riddell

1772 -1808

ward Islands. While there she married Walter Riddell, brother of the poet's friend, Captain Riddell of Glenriddell. Walter bought an estate near Dumfries, which he renamed Woodley Park, in his wife's honour. Maria appears to have been, like Robert, somewhat unconventional and they struck up a strong friendship; indeed her short biography of the poet after his death shows her fitness to have been the official biographer of Burns — rather than Currie, who used poor Robert to spread his own moral tenets — but she was not seriously considered, perhaps solely on grounds of her sex. She described him thus — "... the animated expressions... were almost peculiar to himself;... His voice alone could improve upon the magic of his eye; sonorous, replete with the finest modulations, it alternately captivated the ear with the melody of poetic members, the perspicuity of nervous reasoning, or the ardent sallies of enthusiastic patriotism". They would remain friends for the few years of life left to the poet, although relations became very strained after Burns caused offence to the Riddell family late in 1793.

Burns was promoted to the Dumfries Port Division in February 1792, which he covered on foot and for which he received £70 per annum. Soon after this, he was involved in seizing a smuggler's vessel, the brig *Rosamond* . The excise officers drew up, with a force of Dragoons, into three divisions, one led by the poet and approached the ship under fire from the crew and boarded to find her abandoned. The ship was repaired and the contents sold at public auction, realising £166/16/6d.

Burns bought four carronades for £4 and sent them to the French Convention to show his support for the revolution, a questionable act for a government employee. The guns were intercepted and seized by Customs at Dover. On 11 April, he was made an honorary member of the Royal Company of Archers and Creech suggested a new volume of poems to which Burns offered "about fifty pages" of new material. Creech delayed so long that it didn't appear until almost a year later, containing *Tam O' Shanter* and *Lament for James, Earl of Glencairn.* The volume was reissued in 1794, such was the demand.

Since 1787, Robert had been the unacknowledged editor of James Johnson's *Scots Musical Museum,* taking old Scots songs, many of which were bawdy and transforming them, indeed sometimes completely rewriting them, always leaving his own indelible mark of genius on them, whilst retaining the bawdy for his own *Merry Muses.* In 1792, the fourth volume appeared and a few weeks later George Thomson of Edinburgh proposed a similar venture for which Burns, as with

Johnson, refused payment "...to talk of money, wages, hire, etc. could be downright Sodomy of Soul! — A proof of each of the Songs that I compose or amend, I shall receive as a favour".

The songs which appeared in both volumes represent Burns' greatest gift to Scotland in his outstanding talent for placing verses to airs which would have otherwise been lost or unintelligible. He very quickly sent songs like *The Lea-Rig* and *Duncan Gray*.

Gie me the hour o' gleamin grey—
It maks my heart sae cheery, O,
To meet thee on the lea-rig,
My ain kind dearie, O!

The Lea-Rig, 1792

Here's a freedom to him that was read!
Here's freedom to him that wad write!
There's nane ever fear'd red that the truth should be heard
But they that the truth would indite!

Here's a health to them that's awa

As 1792 progressed, Burns grew less discreet about his political leanings. At a performance of *As You Like It* in Dumfries, when the National Anthem was played, those in the pits called for *Ça Ira*, the French Revolutionary song, while Burns was present, bringing down on him the wrath of his Excise superiors, with the poet protesting his innocence, escaping with a censure. "Dear Christles's Bobby", wrote William Nicol "...what concerns it thee whether the lousy Dumfresian fiddlers play '*Ça Ira*'... "

He would however continue to support the French Revolution, even to the extent, eventually of estranging Mrs Dunlop.

I will fight France with you, Dumourier,
I will take my chance with you, Dumourier,
By my soul, I'll dance with you, Dumourier.
Address to General Dumourier

When Thomson's first volume appeared, he sent a copy to Burns, plus £5, which roused Burns to indignation at this "pecuniary parcel", although the poet congratulated Thomson on the volume's elegant appearance. In September 1793, Burns described his method of composing song to Thomson — "I consider the poetic Sentiment, correspondent to my idea of the musical expression; then chuse my theme; begin one Stanza; when that is composed, which is generally the most difficult part of the business, I walk out, sit down now and then, look out for objects in Nature around me that are in unison or harmony with... the workings of my bosom; ...humming every now and then the air with the verses I have framed; ...I retire to the solitary fireside of my study and there commit my effusions to paper".

He had previously written to confess "I have not that command of the language that I have of my native tongue. In fact I think my ideas are more barren in English than in Scottish".In May 1793 Robert, Jean and family moved to Mill Vennel, now Burns Street; it was to be his last home.

In Christmas week, he estranged himself from Friars' Carse when, after dinner, the party of gentlemen decided to re-enact the rape of the Sabine women with Burns overstepping the mark with his hostess; he was shown the door, never to return. The poet soberly apologised the next day "...from the regions of Hell", to no avail. Whatever the offence was, Burns was never forgiven. A few months later, Robert Riddell died suddenly.

Mine was th' insensate frenzied part,

Ah! why should I such scenes outlive? —

Scenes so abhorrent to my heart!

'Tis thine to pity and forgive.

        Sent to a Gentleman whom he had offended, 1794

In May 1794, Robert turned down an opportunity to leave the Excise to work on the London *Morning Chronicle* as occasional correspondent at a fee of 5 guineas. The move to London had no appeal to the poet, although he did offer "any bagatelle" he might be able to provide. During the summer he toured Galloway

with Syme, spending three days at Ken-
mure Castle with the Jacobite earl and
then visited the Earl of Selkirk at Kirk-
cudbright as guests with the Italian com-
poser Pietro Urbani. While there he composed the famous Selkirk grace —

Some have meat and cannot eat,

Some cannot eat that want it;

But we have meat, and we can eat,

Sae Let the Lord be thankit.

The Selkirk Grace, 1794

The year 1795 was to be one of mixed
fortunes for Burns. Mrs. Dunlop broke off
correspondence with him when he gave
vent to his French Jacobin sentiments to
her. With a son in the army and two
French refugee sons-in law, she was
deeply offended and wrote no more to
him. Burns began to feel the pinch due to
the war and suffered more and more serious bouts of illness. The breach with
Maria Riddell began to heal, however, and
he had a miniature portrait painted by
Reid, saying "I think he has hit by far the

best likeness of me..." Burns was extremely active by now and in addition to his work in the Excise (where he became acting supervisor upon Findlater being ill), his poetry and songwriting, he also joined the newly formed Dumfries Volunteers militia company, perhaps realising, at least in part, his sentiments upon returning to Lochlea from Irvine 13 years later.

O, why the deuce should I repine,
and be an ill foreboder?
I'm twenty-three, and five feet-nine,
I'll go and be a sodger!

I'll go and be a Sodger 1782

It was in 1795 that Burns sent some songs to Thomson, including *Is there for honest poverty*, with the accompanying note "A great critic (Aiken) on songs says that Love and Wine are the exclusive themes for songwriting. This is on neither subject and consequently is no song — ...I do not give ...the song for your book, but merely by way of vive la bagatelle". The song shows Burns' attitude to class division, and is now rightly famous, as a song of hope —

Then let us pray that come it may

As come it will, for a' that —

That Sense and Worth o'er a' the earth

Shall bear the gree an a' that;

For a' that, an a' that,

It's comin yet for a that,

That man to man, the world o'er

Shall brithers be for a' that.

Is there for honest poverty, 1795

In the Spring of 1795 Burns wrote to Maria Riddell saying he was "so ill as to be scarce able to hold this miserable pen to this miserable paper". His daughter Elizabeth was sent to Mossgiel, in the hope that fresher air might revive her from what would prove to be a fatal illness. She died in September, the poet unable to attend her funeral due to pressing excise duties. He suffered a more severe attack of illness which brought him to "the borders of the grave".

On 31 January 1796 he tried once more to make contact with Mrs. Dunlop, sending her the poem, *Does haughty Gaul invasion threat?* with the testimony to his democratic convictions.

...But while we sing, God save the King,
We'll ne'er forget the people!

He told her of his grief at his daughter's death and his own proximity to death, all to no avail. As if all these problems were not enough for his weak condition, Dumfries suffered food shortages

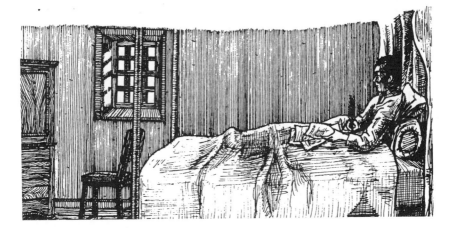

due to the war, with riots in the streets from 12 to 14 March.

With Jean pregnant, an 18-year-old girl named Jessy Lewars stayed to help around the house. Robert wrote one of his most tender love songs to her favourite air *Lennox Love to Blantyre.*

O, wert thou in the cauld blast,

On yonder lea, on yonder lea,

My plaidie to the angry airt,

I'd shelter thee, I'd shelter thee.

Or did Misfortune's bitter storms

Around thee blaw, around thee blaw,

Thy bield should be my bosom

To share it a', to share it a'.

O, wert thou in the cauld blast, 1796

By now his friend Dr. Maxwell was deeply concerned about him, and due to limited medical knowledge of the day (Laennec did not invent the stethoscope until a few years after the poet's death), Maxwell diagnosed Burns' angina as "flying gout", recommending sea-bathing and horse riding. On 3 July, Robert travelled to the hamlet of Brow on the Solway coast and steeped himself in the cold sea-water. The effect on his poor heart was traumatic. On 7 July, Maria who was also recuperating near Brow, sent her carriage for Burns. She was shocked at his appearance, and he said "Well Madam?, and have you any commands for the next world?"

He made a final attempt to contact Mrs Dunlop writing of how he treasured receiving her letters — "The remembrance yet adds one pulse more to my poor palpitating heart". He wrote also to Gilbert of his condition, finishing with "... Remember me to my Mother". The tailor who had made the poet's Volunteer's uniform demanded settlement, striking terror into his already weak heart and Burns wrote

to his cousin James Burness and George Thomson asking to borrow some money.

He had decided to come home the next week and when he did Jean was alarmed at his state of health, while he appealed to James Armour to send his wife to assist Jean — "...I think ...that the disorder will prove fatal to me". On July 20, Syme visited, and left convinced that the end was near. Tradition has it that Burns rallied long enough to say his farewells to his wife and children, before falling into unconsciousness. On 21 July 1796, the poet died, at the age of 37.

His funeral procession was led not only by the Dumfries Volunteers, but by the Cinque Ports Cavalry and Angus Fencibles who were stationed in the town. While the funeral service took place in St Michael's Church overlooking the Nith, Jean gave birth to his son, Maxwell.

Since then, every 25th of January, Burns' birth has been remembered and the now traditional Burns Suppers, which commemorate the poet's life and work are held not only in Scotland but in places as far apart as the USA, Canada and Russia; the poet's fame is now established in the farthest corners of the globe. He could never have imagined it thus.

Jean lived on at the house in Mill Vennel until 1834, when she died. Of Robert's surviving children, Elizabeth (Dear bought Bess), his daughter by Elizabeth Paton, had seven children of her own and died in 1817. Robert junior was educated at Glasgow University and became a civil servant in the Stamp Office in London later to retire to Dumfries where he died, aged 70, in 1857. Francis Wallace died in 1803. William Nicol became a Lieutenant Colonel, later a Colonel in the East India

Company, 7th Native Infantry and died in 1872 in Cheltenham. James Glencairn was also a Lieutenant Colonel, appointed a Judge and Collector in 1833 and died in 1865. The house in Mill Vennel, later renamed Burns Street, has become a shrine for Burnsians while the cottage at Alloway, after some years as a public house, was taken over, whitewashed and stands today as a museum and centre-piece of the Burns country close to the Burns Monument. There are statues of Robert Burns in many of Scotland's cities and larger towns and they can be found as far away as New Zealand. The one which appears on the jacket of this book is by Charles Calverley and stands in Albany, New York in the United States. Even in death, he maintains a steady gaze over the world he left too soon.